FAITH OVER FEAR: OVERING COMING SELF DOUBT AND IMPOSTER SYNDROME

BY GENE L CHEATHAM

Copyright © 2024 by Gene Cheatham
All rights reserved. No part of this book may be reproduced, distributed, or transmitted in any form or by any means, including photocopying, recording, or other electronic or mechanical methods, without the prior written permission of the publisher, except in the case of brief quotations embodied in critical reviews and certain other noncommercial uses permitted by copyright law. For permission requests, write to the publisher, addressed "Attention: Permissions Coordinator," at the address below.

12 & 2 Transformational Coaching
Email: info@12n2coaching.com

Unless otherwise noted, all Scripture quotations are taken from the Holman Christian Standard Bible®, Copyright © 1999, 2000, 2002, 2003, 2009 by Holman Bible Publishers. Used by permission. Holman Christian Standard Bible®, Holman CSB®, and HCSB® are federally registered trademarks of Holman Bible Publishers.

"2 Do not be conformed to this age, but be transformed by the renewing of your mind, so that you may discern what is the good, pleasing, and perfect will of God."

Romans 12:2

Chapter 1: Understanding Self-Doubt and Imposter Syndrome in Entrepreneurship

Recognizing the Signs of Self-Doubt

Every great journey begins with a single step, but self-doubt can make that first step feel like a leap into the unknown. It whispers in your ear, casting shadows over your potential and slowing your progress. But here's the truth: recognizing self-doubt is the first act of courage in overcoming it. As an entrepreneur, especially if you're venturing into business ownership for the first time, understanding and confronting these doubts is crucial. The sooner you can identify them, the sooner you can bring them into the light of God's truth.

Self-doubt often manifests as a quiet but persistent voice in your mind—a voice that questions your worth and abilities. This voice, which we can liken to the flesh, is not from God. When you catch yourself thinking, "I'm not good enough," or "I don't deserve success," understand that these are lies, not divine truths. God's word tells us otherwise. Believing in yourself is not a sin; it is an acknowledgment of the unique gifts and talents that God has placed within you. Replace those negative thoughts with affirmations rooted in faith and truth, reminding yourself that you are fearfully and wonderfully made for this purpose.

Another thief of joy and progress is comparison. In a world overflowing with success stories, it's easy to look at others and feel like you're falling short. But as 2 Corinthians 10:12 warns us, comparing ourselves to others is not wise. God's plan for your life and business is unique, tailor-made for you alone. When you focus on your own journey, you free yourself to grow, flourish, and fulfill the purpose God has set before you. Celebrate the successes of others, but never let their journey diminish your own.

Procrastination and perfectionism are also subtle manifestations of self-doubt. When you find yourself putting off tasks or obsessing over every detail to the point of paralysis, it's often because you're not fully trusting in God's timing and plan. Perfectionism, in particular, can be a heavy burden, convincing you that nothing you do is ever good enough. But here's a hard truth: procrastination is a form of sloth, and James 4:17 reminds us that knowing what is right and failing to act on it is indeed a sin. Let go of the need to control every aspect and instead surrender to God's guidance, trusting that He will provide what you need when you need it.

Lastly, self-doubt often reveals itself through physical and emotional turmoil—feelings of anxiety, stress, and overwhelm can be powerful indicators. These symptoms are more than just feelings; they are signals that something is off balance. As a Christian entrepreneur, it's vital to prioritize self-care, not just for your body and mind, but for your spirit. Seek support from mentors, coaches, or fellow believers who can help you navigate these challenges with faith and resilience. And always remember: God is with you every step of the way. He has promised never to leave you nor forsake you, even in the midst of your business ownership journey.

It is also important to surround yourself with a supportive community of fellow Christian entrepreneurs who can uplift and encourage you on your journey. Being a Christian business owner comes with its own unique set of challenges, and sharing these experiences with those who understand can be both comforting and empowering. By opening up about your struggles and celebrating your victories within this community, you gain valuable insights and fresh perspectives. These relationships are not just a source of strength—they're a reminder of the biblical truth: "Where two or more gather in My name, there am I with them" (Matthew 18:20). In the company of like-minded believers, you find the courage to push past imposter syndrome and rise to new levels of success.

The impact of imposter syndrome on business owners can be profound, but as Christian entrepreneurs, we have the power to overcome it with unwavering faith and confidence in God's plan for our lives. By staying rooted in our faith, surrounding ourselves with a supportive community, and trusting in God's provision, we can combat self-doubt and imposter syndrome. This allows us to step boldly into our true calling as successful business owners. Let us embrace our identity as children of God and pursue our entrepreneurial dreams with the assurance that we are fearfully and wonderfully made for such a time as this.

How Fear Can Hold You Back in Your Entrepreneurial Journey

Fear is a powerful force that can cripple our potential, especially in the realm of entrepreneurship. I often refer to fear as a spirit that opposes God, a tool of the enemy designed to keep us from stepping into the greatness that God has destined for us. For now, let's call fear what it truly is: Satan, the adversary who stands against God. As Christian entrepreneurs, it's vital to recognize that fear is not from God. In fact, Scripture reminds us that "God did not give us a spirit of fear, but of power, love, and sound judgment" (2 Timothy 1:7).

One of the most common fears that can hold us back in our entrepreneurial journey is the fear of failure. This fear makes us doubt our abilities and question whether we truly have what it takes to succeed in the business world. But as Christians, we must remember that God has equipped us with the skills and talents necessary to thrive in our entrepreneurial endeavors. We are not alone in this journey—God is with us every step of the way. Faith in ourselves, bolstered by trust in God's guidance, is the antidote to this fear.

Another fear that often plagues entrepreneurs is the fear of success. Success can bring with it new responsibilities and challenges, and we may worry that we are not deserving of the blessings God has in store for us. Yet, Luke 12:48 teaches us that "to whom much is given, much is required." Embracing success with gratitude and humility allows us to honor God's gifts. Remember, God wants us to prosper and succeed in all areas of our lives, and by accepting His blessings with a grateful heart, we acknowledge His goodness and sovereignty.

Chapter 2: Overcoming Self-Doubt Through Faith

Trusting in God's Plan for Your Business

Trusting in God's plan is the lifeblood of Christian entrepreneurship, especially when faced with self-doubt and imposter syndrome. As first-time business owners, it's easy to feel overwhelmed by the challenges that accompany entrepreneurship. However, when you place your trust in God and His divine plan, you gain the strength to overcome these obstacles with confidence and faith.

God has a unique plan and purpose for each of us, including our businesses. By surrendering control and trusting in His guidance, you can find peace and assurance in your entrepreneurial journey. Remember, God is always with you, leading and guiding you every step of the way. Trust in His timing and provision, knowing that He has a perfect plan for your business's success. As Luke 12:48 reminds us, "For unto whomsoever much is given, of him shall be much required." Embrace the responsibility and the blessings with confidence in God's unwavering support.

When doubt begins to creep in, remember that God has equipped you with everything you need to succeed. He has endowed you with unique talents, skills, and opportunities that are yours alone. By trusting in His plan, you can unlock your full potential and achieve greatness in your business. Have faith in yourself and in God's miraculous power to work in your life.

Imposter syndrome may try to convince you that you're not qualified or capable of running a successful business, but always remember—God does not make mistakes. He has called you to this path for a reason, and He will provide you with the strength and wisdom to overcome any challenges that come your way. Trust in His plan, and believe in yourself, knowing that you are worthy and capable of achieving your entrepreneurial dreams.

In moments of uncertainty and fear, turn to God for guidance and reassurance. Pray for His wisdom and discernment as you navigate the ups and downs of entrepreneurship. Trust in His plan for your business and have faith that He will lead you to success. With God by your side, no challenge is too great, and no dream is too big. Trust in His plan, believe in yourself, and watch as He works wonders in your business and life. As Romans 8:37-39 reminds us:

"No, in all these things we are more than conquerors through him who loved us. For I am convinced that neither death nor life, neither angels nor demons, neither the present nor the future, nor any powers, neither height nor depth, nor anything else in all creation, will be able to separate us from the love of God that is in Christ Jesus our Lord."

Finding Strength in Your Christian Faith

In the world of entrepreneurship, moments of self-doubt and imposter syndrome are inevitable. For a Christian business owner, these feelings can be especially challenging to navigate while staying true to your faith. Yet, it's crucial to remember that your Christian faith is a powerful source of strength and guidance during these uncertain times.

One way to find strength in your faith is to lean on the promises of God. The Bible is rich with verses that remind us of God's faithfulness, love, and provision. When you feel overwhelmed or doubtful, turn to these scriptures for encouragement and reassurance. God has a plan for your life and is with you every step of the way, guiding you through every challenge.

Surrounding yourself with a community of fellow believers is another powerful way to find strength in your faith. Seek out a mentor or join a Christian business group where you can share your struggles and successes with like-minded individuals. Connecting with others who share your faith provides comfort and reminds you that you're not alone in your entrepreneurial journey.

Prayer is an indispensable tool that can bring you peace and strength in your Christian faith. Dedicate time each day to pray for guidance, wisdom, and courage as you face the challenges of entrepreneurship. Trust that God hears your prayers and will equip you with the strength to overcome any obstacles. By surrendering your fears and doubts to God in prayer, you can find peace in knowing that He is in control. One of my favorite stories about the power of prayer is found in the Old Testament when David was surrounded by enemies on all sides. The Bible says that David sought the Lord, and God answered him—not by destroying his enemies, but by removing his fear (Psalm 34:4).

Ultimately, finding strength in your Christian faith means trusting in God's plan for your life and believing that He has equipped you with everything you need to succeed as an entrepreneur. By centering your business on principles of faith, love, and integrity, you can overcome self-doubt and imposter syndrome with confidence and grace. With God on your side, no challenge is too great to overcome. Trust in Him, lean on His promises, and watch as He transforms your fears into faith and your doubts into courage.

In the journey of entrepreneurship, it's easy to fall into the trap of wanting to control every aspect of our businesses. We want to dictate every outcome, plan every detail, and ensure that everything goes according to our own desires. However, as Christian entrepreneurs, we must remember that true success comes from surrendering to God's will. When we let go of control and trust in His plan for our lives and businesses, we open ourselves to endless possibilities and blessings that we could never have imagined on our own.

Surrendering to God's will requires deep faith and trust in His timing and purpose for our lives. It means letting go of our limited understanding and embracing His infinite wisdom and guidance. When we release our need for control and place our business in His hands, we allow Him to work miracles in ways that we could never achieve on our own. His plans for us are always good, even when they don't align with our expectations.

As Christian entrepreneurs, we must also let go of the fear and self-doubt that often accompany the entrepreneurial journey. It's easy to feel overwhelmed and inadequate, especially when facing challenges and setbacks. However, when we surrender to God's will, we find peace and confidence in knowing that He is always with us, guiding and supporting us every step of the way. Trust in His promises and rest assured that He will never leave you nor forsake you.

Letting Go of Control and Surrendering to God's Will

Letting go of control and surrendering to God's will opens the door to true freedom and joy in our businesses. When we release our grip on the reins and place our trust in Him, we shed the heavy burdens of self-doubt and imposter syndrome that can hinder us from reaching our full potential. By embracing the unique gifts and talents God has bestowed upon us, we can move forward with confidence, knowing that He has equipped us for success and will guide us to fulfill our purpose with grace and assurance.

Proverbs 3:5-6 reminds us to "Trust in the Lord with all your heart and lean not on your own understanding; in all your ways acknowledge Him, and He will make your paths straight." True success comes when we fully surrender to God's will. By letting go of control and placing our trust in His divine plan for our lives and businesses, we open ourselves to endless possibilities and blessings. As we release our fears and doubts, placing our faith in Him, we experience a profound sense of freedom, joy, and fulfillment in our entrepreneurial journey. Let us wholeheartedly embrace His will for our lives and businesses, confident that He is always by our side, guiding us toward greatness.

CHAPTER 3 Building Confidence and Resilience as a Christian Entrepreneur

Embracing Your Unique Gifts and Talents

Embracing the unique gifts and talents God has given you is essential on your journey as a Christian entrepreneur. Each of us is endowed with special talents and skills meant to be used for His glory. Whether it's a talent for problem-solving, a knack for connecting with others, or a creative mind that sees opportunities where others see obstacles, these are valuable assets that set you apart in the business world.

When you fully embrace your unique gifts and talents, you empower yourself and inspire others to do the same. As a Christian entrepreneur, you have the opportunity to break barriers and pave the way for others who may be hesitant to pursue their entrepreneurial dreams. By confidently owning your gifts and talents, you demonstrate that it is possible to overcome self-doubt and imposter syndrome and achieve success in the business world.

Romans 12:6 reminds us that "God has given each of us the ability to do certain things well." Embracing your unique gifts and talents is not only essential for your own success but also for the impact you can have on others. By trusting in God's plan for your life and recognizing the special gifts He has given you, you can overcome your fears and build a thriving business that reflects your true purpose and passion. Remember, you are fearfully and wonderfully made, and your gifts are meant to be shared with the world.

Setting Realistic Goals and Celebrating Small Wins

In the journey of entrepreneurship, it's easy to become overwhelmed by the big picture and lose sight of the small victories along the way. However, by setting realistic goals and taking the time to celebrate each milestone, you can build confidence and momentum in your entrepreneurial journey.

As Christian entrepreneurs, it's important to remember that God has a plan for our lives and our businesses. By setting realistic goals that align with our values and beliefs, we can trust that we are on the right path toward fulfilling our purpose. When we commit our work to the Lord and seek His guidance, He provides us with the strength and wisdom to achieve our goals.

Proverbs 16:3 tells us to "Commit your works to the Lord, and your thoughts will be established." Celebrating small wins is an essential part of building confidence and overcoming self-doubt in entrepreneurship. Each achievement, no matter how small, is a step toward success and deserves to be recognized. Whether it's landing a new client, reaching a sales target, or launching a product, each victory is worth celebrating.

By focusing on setting realistic goals and celebrating small wins, we can break down our larger vision into manageable tasks and stay motivated along the way. The Bible reminds us that even the smallest acts of faith can lead to great miracles. By trusting in God's plan for our businesses and celebrating each step of the journey, we can overcome self-doubt and imposter syndrome and achieve our entrepreneurial dreams.

Overall, setting realistic goals and celebrating small wins are necessary practices for Christian entrepreneurs. By aligning our goals with our faith and values, seeking guidance from God, and taking the time to acknowledge and celebrate our achievements, we can build confidence, momentum, and success in our businesses. Remember, even the smallest steps forward are progress toward our ultimate goals, and each victory, no matter how small, is worth celebrating. Trust in God's plan for your business, have faith in yourself, and keep moving forward, one small win at a time.

Surrounding Yourself with a Supportive Community of Like-Minded Individuals

As Christian entrepreneurs, it's vital to remember that we are not alone on this journey. Surrounding ourselves with a supportive community of like-minded individuals can make all the difference. Having a strong community of people who share your values and beliefs can provide the support and encouragement needed to overcome fears and move forward in your entrepreneurial endeavors.

Navigating the business world while staying true to your faith can be challenging. However, by surrounding yourself with a supportive community of like-minded individuals, you gain access to the guidance and wisdom needed to stay grounded in your beliefs while pursuing your entrepreneurial goals. This community can help you stay focused on your faith, offer encouragement during difficult times, and celebrate your successes alongside you.

In the end, entrepreneurship is not just about building a business; it's about building a life that reflects your faith and values. By letting go of control, embracing your unique gifts, setting realistic goals, celebrating small wins, and surrounding yourself with a supportive community, you can overcome self-doubt and imposter syndrome, and achieve your entrepreneurial dreams while staying true to your Christian faith.

Chapter 4: Cultivating a Positive Mindset for Business Success

Practicing Thankfulness and Mindfulness in Your Daily Routine

In the fast-paced world of entrepreneurship, it's easy to get swept away by the pressures and challenges that arise each day. Yet, as Christian entrepreneurs, we hold a secret weapon: the power of thankfulness and mindfulness. These practices are not just nice-to-haves; they are essential tools for cultivating a resilient mindset, one that can withstand the storms of self-doubt and imposter syndrome.

Imagine starting each day with a heart full of gratitude. By taking just a moment to acknowledge the blessings in your life, both big and small, you begin to shift your focus. You move from a mindset of scarcity to one of abundance, recognizing that everything you need is already within your grasp, provided by a loving and faithful God. This daily practice can be as simple as offering a prayer of thanks as you rise, acknowledging the opportunities, resources, and connections that God has placed in your path.

But thankfulness is only part of the equation. Mindfulness—being fully present in the moment—completes it. In the hustle of running a business, it's easy to become consumed by worries about the future or regrets about the past. Mindfulness anchors you in the now, allowing you to truly experience life as it unfolds. It empowers you to recognize and challenge the negative thoughts that creep in, undermining your confidence. By cultivating mindfulness, you become more aware of the narrative running through your mind, giving you the power to rewrite it with God's truth.

When gratitude and mindfulness become part of your daily routine, they transform your inner landscape. They help you create a sanctuary of peace and contentment within yourself, a place where you can retreat when the external world becomes overwhelming. This internal peace is your shield against the challenges of entrepreneurship, allowing you to navigate your business journey with grace and resilience. You are not alone in this journey; God is walking with you, guiding you, and providing you with the strength you need to succeed.

As you incorporate these practices into your life, remember that they are more than just tools—they are acts of faith. By practicing gratitude and mindfulness, you deepen your connection to God, trust in His plan, and strengthen your resolve to overcome any obstacle. So, take a moment each day to count your blessings, center your mind, and remember that with God by your side, you are unstoppable.

Overcoming Negative Self-Talk and Limiting Beliefs

"For as he thinketh in his heart, so is he." — Proverbs 23:7

In the journey of entrepreneurship, one of the greatest battles we face is within our own minds. Negative self-talk and limiting beliefs are like dark clouds that obscure our vision, making us doubt our capabilities and question our worth. But as Christian entrepreneurs, we are called to rise above these thoughts, to walk in the confidence that comes from knowing who we are in Christ. It's time to break free from the chains of self-doubt and step boldly into the purpose that God has for us.

Negative self-talk is a thief. It steals our joy, our confidence, and our ability to see ourselves as God sees us—capable, chosen, and equipped for greatness. It whispers lies like "You're not good enough," "You're not smart enough," or "You'll never succeed." But these are not the words of our Creator. God speaks life, hope, and promise into our existence. When we allow negative self-talk to dominate our minds, we are choosing to believe the enemy's lies over God's truth.

Limiting beliefs are like invisible chains, holding us back from reaching our full potential. They are the false narratives we've internalized over time, often based on past experiences or the opinions of others. But as followers of Christ, we are called to break these chains. Remember, Jesus is the ultimate chain breaker. He came to set us free from every lie, every fear, and every limitation. When we align our thoughts with His truth, we unlock the doors to our destiny.

Imposter syndrome is a particularly insidious form of self-doubt, especially among first-time business owners and minorities. It's that nagging feeling that you don't belong, that you're not qualified, that you're just pretending to know what you're doing. But here's the truth: You are not an imposter. You are a child of God, fearfully and wonderfully made, called to walk in purpose and authority. Your identity is not defined by your achievements or your failures, but by the One who created you.

As Christian entrepreneurs, we must remember that faith is greater than fear. We must overcome negative self-talk and limiting beliefs with the power of God's Word. Speak life over yourself. Replace those lies with affirmations rooted in Scripture. Declare, "I am fearfully and wonderfully made," "I can do all things through Christ who strengthens me," and "Greater is He that is in me than he that is in the world." When we speak God's truth over our lives, we align ourselves with His will, and we position ourselves for success.

Using Affirmations to Manifest Your Dreams

Affirmations are powerful declarations that can transform your life and business. They are not just empty words; they are expressions of faith that align your heart and mind with God's promises. As you journey through the ups and downs of entrepreneurship, affirmations can be the anchor that keeps you grounded in truth and focused on your goals.

Start each day by speaking life over yourself and your business. Declare your worth, your abilities, and your potential for success. Say, "I am equipped for every good work," "I am a vessel of God's creativity and wisdom," and "My business is blessed and highly favored." These affirmations are more than just positive thinking—they are statements of faith that invite God's power and favor into your life.

Remember to root your affirmations in Scripture. The Bible is full of promises that you can claim for your life and business. By aligning your affirmations with God's Word, you are not just speaking positive words—you are declaring God's truth over your life. This is the key to manifesting your dreams as a Christian entrepreneur.

As you incorporate affirmations into your daily routine, stay connected to God through prayer and Scripture. Seek His guidance as you navigate the challenges of entrepreneurship. Trust in His plan for your life and business, and take bold action towards your goals. With God's strength and favor on your side, there is nothing that can stand in the way of your success. Embrace the power of affirmations and watch as your dreams unfold in ways you never imagined.

In summary, cultivating a positive mindset is crucial for business success. By practicing thankfulness and mindfulness, overcoming negative self-talk and limiting beliefs, and using affirmations to manifest your dreams, you can overcome self-doubt and imposter syndrome. You can step confidently into the purpose that God has for you. Trust in His plan, believe in your abilities, and take bold action towards your goals. With God by your side, you are destined for greatness.

Chapter 5: Taking Action and Stepping Out in Faith

Pushing Past Your Comfort Zone and Taking Risks

As Christian entrepreneurs, we're called to step out in faith, leaving behind the comfort of the familiar and embracing the unknown. The path of entrepreneurship is paved with risks and challenges, yet it is also where we find the most growth. Just as Peter stepped out of the boat to walk on water, we, too, must dare to step beyond our comfort zones, even when the winds howl and the waves crash around us. It's in these moments that we discover the strength God has placed within us, a strength that equips us to face and overcome every obstacle.

For first-time business owners, the fear of failure and self-doubt can feel paralyzing. However, we must remember that failure is not the end—it's a stepping stone toward success. Each risk taken is an act of faith, a declaration that we trust God's plan for our lives. By stepping out of our comfort zones, we open ourselves to new opportunities and experiences that can lead us closer to our dreams.

The journey of entrepreneurship requires us to embrace uncertainty and trust that God is with us every step of the way. The world may tell us to play it safe, but as followers of Christ, we are called to be bold, to take risks, and to walk in faith. Let us push past our fears, knowing that with God, all things are possible. As we venture into the unknown, we do so not alone but with the assurance that God's hand is there to guide us, just as He was there for Peter on the water.

"Remember ye not the former things, neither consider the things of old. Behold, I will do a new thing; now shall it spring forth; shall ye not know it? I will even make a way in the wilderness, and rivers in the desert."
Isaiah 43:18-19

Embracing Failure as a Learning Opportunity

In the world of entrepreneurship, failure is not something to be feared; it is a powerful teacher. As Christian entrepreneurs, we must shift our perspective on failure and see it as an essential part of the journey. Each setback is an opportunity to learn, to grow, and to refine our approach. When we embrace failure with the right mindset, we turn it into a stepping stone toward our ultimate success.

Failure is not a reflection of our worth or abilities; it reflects our willingness to take risks and push ourselves beyond the limits of our comfort zones. Every great success story is filled with moments of failure, yet it is through these failures that the seeds of future success are planted. By analyzing what went wrong and why, we can adjust and improvements that will serve us well in the future.

As Christian entrepreneurs, it is vital to remember that our identity is not defined by our achievements or our failures. Our worth is rooted in Christ, who calls us to walk in confidence and purpose. When we embrace failure as a learning opportunity, we break free from the chains of imposter syndrome and self-doubt. We step forward with the knowledge that each failure brings us closer to the success that God has planned for us.

"A righteous person may fall seven times, but he gets up again. However, in a disaster, wicked people fall."
Proverbs 24:16

Trusting in God's Guidance as You Navigate the Challenges of Entrepreneurship

The journey of entrepreneurship is filled with challenges that can test our faith and resolve. It is easy to become overwhelmed by self-doubt and imposter syndrome, especially as a first-time business owner. However, when we trust in God's plan for our lives and businesses, we gain the strength and wisdom needed to overcome any obstacle.

God has a unique purpose for each of us, and that includes our entrepreneurial endeavors. By seeking His guidance through prayer and scripture, we align ourselves with His will and find the courage to face even the most daunting challenges. When setbacks occur, we can find comfort in knowing that God's plan is greater than our fears. He is with us, guiding and supporting us every step of the way.

Trusting in God's guidance also means surrounding ourselves with a supportive community of like-minded individuals. Other Christian business owners can offer valuable insights and encouragement as we navigate the ups and downs of entrepreneurship. We are not alone on this journey—God has placed people in our lives to help us succeed.

As we step out in faith, let us do so with the confidence that God is in control. He knows the path ahead, and He will guide us through every challenge. Trust in His promises, and you will find the faith to overcome any obstacle that comes your way. Remember, with God on our side, success is not just possible; it is inevitable.

"A man's steps are established by the Lord, and He takes pleasure in his way. Though he falls, he will not be overwhelmed, because the Lord holds his hand."
Psalm 37:23-24

Chapter 6: Empowering Others Through Your Story of Faith Over Fear

Unleashing the Power of Your Testimony

Your story is your greatest weapon. As a Christian entrepreneur, your journey through self-doubt and imposter syndrome holds the potential to transform lives. It's not just about your victory; it's about the impact your testimony can have on others who are standing where you once stood. You've felt the weight of uncertainty, the whispers of inadequacy, and the fear of stepping into the unknown. But by God's grace, you've emerged stronger, more resilient, and emboldened by faith.

Imagine this: Someone is on the brink of giving up, crushed by the belief that they are not enough. Then they hear your story—a story of struggle, yes, but more importantly, a story of triumph. A story that tells them, "You can make it too." Your testimony is a lighthouse in the storm, guiding others to safe harbor. It's a living testament that with God, nothing is impossible.

Faith Over Fear: A Call to Rise Above

Fear is a formidable enemy, especially for first-time entrepreneurs. The fear of failure, of not being enough, can paralyze even the most passionate hearts. But as you stand in your truth, declaring that your faith is greater than your fear, you become a beacon of hope. Your journey isn't just yours—it's a lifeline to those who are drowning in self-doubt.

Every step you've taken, every hurdle you've overcome, is a testimony to the power of faith. You weren't just conquering your fears for yourself; you were paving the way for others. When you share your story, you tell others, "If I can do it, so can you." You become the voice that cuts through the noise of doubt and fear, inspiring others to take that first bold step toward their dreams.

Igniting the Flame in Fellow Entrepreneurs

In the world of entrepreneurship, self-doubt and imposter syndrome are insidious foes. But what if your story could be the spark that ignites a fire in someone else? What if, by sharing your journey, you could help others see their own worth and potential? As Christian entrepreneurs, we are called to lift each other up, to be the iron that sharpens iron.

This journey isn't meant to be walked alone. In community, we find strength, encouragement, and the affirmation that we are not defined by our failures. By sharing our stories, we create a ripple effect of empowerment. Your story, your voice, can become the catalyst for someone else's breakthrough. When you share how you've overcome, you remind others that they too have what it takes. You become a living, breathing example of God's faithfulness and power.

Creating a Legacy of Faith and Resilience

The legacy you leave isn't just in the profits you make or the accolades you receive. It's in the lives you touch, the hope you restore, and the faith you ignite in others. As Christian entrepreneurs, we have a unique opportunity to build something far greater than ourselves—a legacy of faith, resilience, and empowerment that will echo through generations.

Think of the future entrepreneurs who will look to your story as a blueprint for their own success. By sharing your journey of overcoming fear and self-doubt, you are giving them a gift—a roadmap to navigate their own challenges. You are telling them, "You are not alone. You are capable. You are chosen by God to do great things."

Our businesses become more than just enterprises; they become platforms for change, places where others can find the courage to step into their God-given purpose. By leading with faith, by choosing to walk in resilience, we show others that with God, all things are possible. This is the inheritance we leave: not just wealth, but wisdom; not just success, but significance.

"A good person leaves an inheritance for their children's children, but the sinner's wealth is laid up for the righteous." **Proverbs 13:22**

Embracing Your Identity as a Fearless Christian Entrepreneur

This is your moment. It's time to stand tall and declare your identity as a fearless Christian entrepreneur. The world may tell you that you're not enough, that your dreams are too big, that your faith is too small. But those are lies. The truth is that you are fearfully and wonderfully made, equipped by God for every good work.

As you face the challenges of entrepreneurship, remember who you are—a child of the King, called to walk by faith and not by sight. Your fears may be loud, but your faith is louder. Embrace your identity as a fearless Christian entrepreneur, knowing that God is with you every step of the way.

Surround yourself with a community that believes in you, that speaks life into your dreams, that prays for your success. Together, we can conquer any fear, overcome any obstacle, and achieve success that not only fulfills us but glorifies God.

So, stand up and boldly declare: "I am a fearless Christian entrepreneur. I trust in God's plan for my life. I embrace my identity and surround myself with a community of believers. I stand on the foundation of faith, knowing that I can conquer any fear and achieve success in my entrepreneurial endeavors. I am "fearfully and wonderfully made", and I am deeply loved by God.

This is your story. Own it. Share it. Let it be the light that leads others out of the darkness and into the abundant life God has planned for them.

Final Chapter: Fearless Faith: Your Blueprint for Christian Entrepreneurship

As you reach the conclusion of this book, I want to leave you with one final message: You are called to be fearless. The journey of entrepreneurship is fraught with challenges—self-doubt, imposter syndrome, and fear—but you have within you the power to overcome them all through your faith in God.

Embrace the Fear and Move Forward
Fear is a natural part of the entrepreneurial journey, but it doesn't have to hold you back. Instead, see it as a stepping stone—an opportunity for growth. Remember, "For God has not given us a

spirit of fear, but of power and of love and of a sound mind" (2 Timothy 1:7). Lean into your faith, trust in His guidance, and take bold steps forward, knowing that He is with you every step of the way.

The Power of a Faith-Driven Mindset
Your mindset is the cornerstone of your success. By cultivating a mindset rooted in faith, gratitude, and resilience, you can rise above the challenges that come your way. "And we know that in all things God works for the good of those who love him, who have been called according to his purpose" (Romans 8:28). Practice daily affirmations, set realistic goals, and celebrate each small victory. Surround yourself with a community of like-minded believers who will support and uplift you on this journey.

A Planner to Guide Your Path
To further support you, I've created a planner designed specifically for Christian entrepreneurs like you. This isn't just a tool—it's a spiritual guide, helping you align your business goals with your faith. "Commit to the LORD whatever you do, and he will establish your plans" (Proverbs 16:3). With daily scriptures, goal-setting templates, and reflective space, this planner will keep you grounded and focused on God's purpose for your life and business.

Leaving a Legacy of Faith
Your journey doesn't end here. As you continue to grow and succeed, think about the legacy you want to leave behind. "Let your light shine before others, that they may see your good deeds and glorify your Father in heaven" (Matthew 5:16). Share your story of overcoming fear and doubt with others. Mentor and inspire the next generation of Christian entrepreneurs. Your testimony has the power to encourage others to step out in faith and pursue their God-given dreams.

Conclusion: Stepping into Your Calling

You are not just an entrepreneur; you are a vessel for God's work in the world. "I can do all things through Christ who strengthens me" (Philippians 4:13). Embrace your identity as a fearless Christian entrepreneur, knowing that with God's guidance, you can achieve more than you ever imagined. Let your faith be the foundation of your business, and let your business be a testament to God's glory.

As you move forward, keep this truth in your heart: "With God, all things are possible" (Matthew 19:26). Now is the time to step out in faith, conquer your fears, and build a business that honors Him.

If you have not yet fully embraced the love and guidance of Jesus Christ in your life, I invite you to do so now. Surrender your heart to Him, and let Him lead your path. Jesus offers a life of purpose, fulfillment, and peace that no worldly success can provide. Accept His love, and allow His grace to transform not only your business but your entire life.

A Simple Prayer of Faith: "Lord Jesus, I believe that You are the Son of God and that You have a plan for my life. I ask for Your guidance as I step into the calling You've placed on my heart. I surrender my business, my fears, and my dreams to You. Strengthen me, fill me with Your Holy Spirit, and lead me as I walk in faith. Thank You for Your love and sacrifice. Amen."

Resource Page

If you're looking for additional support on your journey as a Christian entrepreneur, I encourage you to visit 12 & 2 Transformational Coaching. Through 12 & 2 Coaching, we offer guidance rooted in biblical principles, helping you grow both personally and professionally. Whether you're starting a business, seeking to overcome self-doubt, or aiming to unlock your potential, we are here to walk alongside you.

At 12 & 2 Coaching, we believe that your story is a powerful tool for transformation, and that with God, you can achieve more than you ever imagined. Explore our tailored programs, including leadership development, career pivots, and business growth strategies, all centered on faith and resilience.

Remember, you are not alone on this journey. Together, we can turn your fear into faith and your vision into reality.

Sources and Acknowledgments

Primary Biblical Source:

- **Holman Christian Standard Bible (HCSB)**
  The HCSB is a trusted modern English translation of the Bible, known for its accuracy and readability. It has been used throughout this book to reference key scriptures that guide Christian entrepreneurs in faith and business.
  For more information, visit Holman Christian Standard Bible.

Additional Resources:

- **12 & 2 Transformational Coaching**
  Many of the coaching principles and business strategies shared in this book are inspired by the work we do at **12 & 2 Transformational Coaching**. Rooted in biblical principles, 12 & 2 helps Christian entrepreneurs overcome fear and self-doubt to build thriving businesses.
  Learn more at 12 & 2 Coaching.

- **Faith-Based Entrepreneurial Wisdom**
  The concepts of resilience, surrender to God's will, and stepping out in faith draw heavily from decades of wisdom within the Christian business community, personal experience, and scriptural study. A special acknowledgement goes out to the countless Christian business owners who have shared their journeys and testimonies, providing invaluable insight into what it means to serve both God and community through entrepreneurship.

- **Acknowledgments:**

- To God, for His unwavering guidance and the strength to write this book. Every word is dedicated to Him and His glory.
- To my family, friends, and spiritual mentors who supported me through this writing process.
- To the readers, who have embarked on this journey of faith over fear. May this book inspire you to live out your God-given calling.

www.ingramcontent.com/pod-product-compliance
Lightning Source LLC
Chambersburg PA
CBHW070959220526
45471CB00007B/3098